# A Patient's Guide to Ketamine Therapy

By Patrick Diedrich

Copyright

© 2026 Patrick Diedrich
All rights reserved.

No part of this publication may be reproduced, stored, or transmitted in any form or by any means, electronic or mechanical, without prior written permission of the author, except for brief quotations used in reviews, academic citation, or clinical and educational contexts.

This book is intended for informational and educational purposes only. It does not constitute medical advice and is not a substitute for diagnosis, treatment, or care by a licensed medical professional or licensed mental health clinician in any country or jurisdiction. Ketamine therapy should only be undertaken under appropriate medical supervision and in accordance with applicable local laws and clinical guidelines. The author is not a clinician, and the content reflects personal experience in conjunction with a qualified mental health professional, combined with publicly available research.

Individual responses to ketamine therapy vary. No outcomes are guaranteed. If distress, confusion, or adverse effects occur, readers should contact their treating provider or appropriate medical professional.

Provider Use Notice
Licensed medical and mental health providers may reproduce or distribute this guide in whole or in part for non-commercial clinical use, patient education, or in-office distribution, provided the content is not altered and proper attribution is maintained. No endorsement or affiliation is implied.

First edition

ISBN: 979-8-9945513-0-1

Published by
Patrick Diedrich Press
United States of America

For rights, permissions, or clinical distribution inquiries:
patrickdiedrichpress@gmail.com

# Medical and Safety Disclaimer

This guide is a personal account paired with general educational information. It is not medical advice, nor does it replace integration with a mental health provider. Ketamine therapy should only be undertaken under the supervision of a licensed medical professional. Dosing, delivery method, screening criteria, risks, and expected outcomes vary by individual.

Nothing in this guide should be used to diagnose, treat, or replace care from a qualified provider. If something you experience feels unsafe, confusing, or distressing, contact your provider immediately, or call 911.

# Purpose of This Guide

This book exists because I was once like you, anxious about embarking on an experience I had no frame of reference for. Any time you face something unknown, you may become fearful, nervous, or even excited. The same holds true for a form of therapy that starts by altering your consciousness. Perhaps reading about my journey will alleviate your own worries.

I completed a full six-session IV ketamine protocol. What follows is not a success story, a warning story, or a promise of relief. It is a grounded account of what the process felt like from the inside, paired with practical guidance meant to reduce fear and help you make sense of what happens afterward.

This guide does not ask you to believe anything. It does not ask you to "surrender," "let go," or "trust the universe." It assumes you are thoughtful, cautious, and paying attention.

# Session One: Into the Unknown

No amount of reading or watching online videos will fully prepare you for the first session.

You may feel calm on the surface while tension hums underneath, skeptical and hopeful at the same time. You may also feel nothing at all and quietly wonder if that absence means something is wrong.

For me, the dominant feeling was alert uncertainty. I trusted my provider and understood the protocol, yet I still did not know what it would feel like to lose familiar mental reference points while remaining conscious.

That gap between knowing what was going to happen, and experiencing it for myself, is where my first-session anxiety lived.

On the day of the first ketamine infusion, I was asked to lie down on a padded examination table in the clinic and get as comfortable as possible. As the IV was inserted, my provider handed me a sleep mask and a set of noise-canceling headphones.

Once my eyes were covered and the headphones settled in place, the lights were dimmed and a track began to play, an aetheric mix of binaural beats, natural sounds, and isochronic tones.

This was the point at which the ketamine entered the IV line.

The onset was gradual, with no sharp line separating ordinary awareness from altered awareness.

At some point, the usual sense of my body receded. Thoughts became less verbal and more abstract. Images did not arrive as scenes or memories. They arrived as abstract shapes, movement, and texture.

There was no narrative. No message. No insight delivered in a clean sentence by some interdimensional being.

Time behaved strangely. Minutes stretched, then collapsed in on themselves. Trying to track it made no sense, so I stopped trying.

At some moments it felt like my body was sinking into the table. At others, it felt as though it was soaring on the winds of space and time.

I did not feel euphoric. I did not feel frightened. I felt unanchored.

When the infusion ended, awareness returned in layers. First the room. Then my body. Then language. I had to move carefully. The immediate aftereffects were similar to having a few drinks, without the negative consequences.

I felt alert and energized, but without a clear direction for that energy. There was a sense that something had shifted without knowing what that shift was for. An acute sense of purpose surfaced in my mind, and laser-like focus, but no obvious target for it.

Inside, I felt a calm that was almost unfamiliar at this point in my life. It felt as though the fist of anxiety, which had been clutching my chest for so long that I had assumed it was normal, had finally released. I felt like I had been placed on an even keel for the first time, in a very long time.

I also found sugary snacks extremely satisfying.

## After the Session

Any structured integration work should be guided by your medical or mental health provider. What follows is not a substitute for that guidance, but a reminder to give your nervous system time to settle before drawing conclusions.

In the first day or two, doing less is often more helpful than doing more. Avoid the urge to extract meaning too quickly. Interpretation tends to become clearer once the initial effects have stabilized.

In the first 48 hours, it may help to:
- Maintain predictable routines
- Eat regularly and hydrate
- Limit intense conversations
- Avoid major decisions

Pay attention without interrogating the experience.

## What Research Suggests

Ketamine's antidepressant and anti-trauma effects are associated with changes in glutamate signaling and downstream neuroplastic processes, particularly within prefrontal and limbic circuits [1–3]. Early infusions appear to increase neural flexibility rather than resolve symptoms outright [3,5].

Clinical studies suggest that subjective experiences during initial sessions vary widely, and that meaningful symptom reduction often emerges across repeated treatments rather than immediately after the first infusion [1,2,4].

In simple terms, the first session introduces neural fluidity. Later sessions make use of it [3,5].

# Session Two: Memory

The second session carried a different weight.

I had a reference point now. I knew I would remain conscious, that the room would come back, that the experience would end. That knowledge can reduce fear. It can also make room for anticipation.

For me, this seemed to be the point where emotional material began to surface. Not because the treatment suddenly became stronger, but because my nervous system was less guarded.

I went in expecting something similar to the first session. That expectation did not hold.

This time, part of the experience organized itself around a memory. Not memory in the sense of replaying a clear scene, but memory as emotional recall.

Images became more recognizable. A childhood environment surfaced, not as a complete story, but as fragments. Tone. Color. A brief glimpse of a place. A sense of being small and alert. The emotional charge was stronger than the imagery itself.

Coming out of the session, I felt unsettled and quiet.

There was no relief or clarity, just a large question hanging in the background.

This is a common response when memory or trauma-related material emerges without resolution. Ketamine can surface content without immediately organizing or resolving it. The absence of closure can feel disappointing, or even discouraging.

## After the Session

This is not the moment to force meaning. Focus instead on containment.

After sessions where memory or emotion comes forward without resolution, the nervous system often needs more quiet than insight. Trying to explain or interpret what surfaced too quickly can add strain rather than clarity.

In the first day or two, it can help to:

- Keep social exposure low
- Write factual observations rather than interpretations
- Ground the body through light movement or warm showers
- Speak with your provider if distress lingers beyond a few days

Avoid revisiting traumatic material alone in detail unless you already have therapeutic support in place.

## What Research Suggests

Ketamine is known to disrupt rigid neural patterns while temporarily increasing communication between brain regions that do not usually interact as freely [3,5]. This shift can allow emotionally encoded memories to arise without the usual suppression mechanisms [6,7].

Clinical literature notes that trauma-related recall may appear during early to mid-treatment sessions, sometimes without immediate symptom relief [4,6]. Therapeutic benefit appears to correlate more strongly with cumulative treatment effects than with any single subjective experience [2,5].

Emotional activation during ketamine treatment is not the same as retraumatization, but it should be monitored and discussed with a provider, particularly when distress persists beyond the acute treatment window [4,7].

# Session Three: Silence

By the third session, expectations tend to solidify.

You may expect a pattern to continue, or you may expect escalation. A memory-heavy session can lead you to brace for more. A lighter one can make you look for confirmation that things are moving in the right direction.

I went in alert and curious, carrying a quiet assumption that something would happen.

That assumption turned out to be the main thing that did not belong in the room.

This time, very little occurred in any dramatic sense. There were no strong images, no memories, no emotional surge. Awareness felt flattened and neutral. Thoughts appeared and dissolved without pulling me anywhere.

The experience felt almost procedural.

At moments I wondered if the dose was lower, if something had malfunctioned, or if my brain was somehow resisting the process. Those thoughts came and went. Nothing replaced them.

The session ended without incident.

The dominant feeling afterward was melancholy. Not sadness tied to a story. Not grief. Just a low, persistent heaviness without an obvious cause. That feeling lingered.

There was also a subtle frustration. After the vividness of the first two sessions, this one felt empty. That emptiness made it tempting to label the experience as unproductive.

That label would have been premature.

## After the Session

Muted sessions can be unsettling precisely because they offer so little to react to.

After a quiet or neutral experience, it helps to resist the urge to correct or compensate for what did not happen. Chasing intensity can add pressure where patience is more useful.

In the days that follow, it can help to:
- Maintain regular sleep habits, even if mood feels flat
- Avoid treating neutrality as failure
- Continue light journaling without trying to generate insight
- Notice mood shifts across days rather than hours

If melancholy deepens or becomes impairing, bring it to your provider's attention. Transient mood changes should be tracked rather than ignored.

## What Research Suggests

Ketamine's therapeutic effects do not depend on consistent or vivid conscious experiences [3,5]. Neuroplastic changes associated with treatment can occur without noticeable imagery, emotional activation, or insight [3,6].

Clinical studies describe a wide range of subjective responses across sessions, including periods of emotional flatness or apparent neutrality [1,2]. These phases may reflect transitional states as neural networks reorganize, rather than a lack of therapeutic effect [5,6].

In other words, absence of experience is still an experience. The brain may be recalibrating quietly in the background [3,5].

# Session Four: Release

By the fourth session, the treatment no longer feels new.

You know how your body responds. You know the routine. You know the medication will wear off. Familiarity can bring relief, but it can also expose subtler reactions that novelty may have masked earlier.

I went in without strong expectations, which turned out to be useful.

During the treatment itself, the experience was active but not dramatic. Abstract images appeared and dissolved. Sensations shifted. Awareness moved without settling anywhere for long. There was no central theme, no memory, no emotional peak.

Nothing felt threatening. Nothing felt particularly meaningful. It was simply happening. The low, lingering sadness from the third session remained present but unchanged.

I did not journal until a few days after the fourth treatment. When I did, I decided to focus on where I had felt that particular sadness before. I wrote about other periods in my life marked by the same quiet heaviness. Several instances surfaced quickly, faster than I expected.

After I finished writing, I closed my notebook, went to the kitchen, and made myself lunch.

Sitting at the table maybe ten minutes later, I began to cry without a clear trigger. Not a restrained release, but a full, physical sobbing that arrived without warning. I was not thinking about the journal entry or any specific memory. I was simply eating and listening to something on television.

That moment surprised me more than any ketamine-induced imagery had.

There was no storyline attached. No looping thoughts. Just

release.

With distance, this stands out as an important turning point. Not because it solved anything, but because it loosened something that had been held for a long time. It reinforced the sense that even when feelings are suppressed, they are not erased. If they are not given space later, they may surface in ways that feel stranger or less contained. Letting them move through, when they finally do, matters.

## After the Session

Emotional responses do not always arrive on schedule.

When feelings surface hours or days later, the most helpful response is often to make room for them rather than explain them. Delayed reactions are not a sign that something was missed.

After a delayed emotional release, it can help to:
- Pause and allow the emotion without interruption
- Ground physically through movement or tactile actions
- Avoid judging the timing or intensity of the response
- Write down what occurred in simple, factual terms

If emotional release feels overwhelming or destabilizing, reach out to your provider or a trusted clinician.

## What Research Suggests

Ketamine influences not only conscious perception, but also autonomic and emotional regulation systems [5,6]. Changes in affective processing can emerge after the acute dissociative effects have resolved [6,8].

Clinical literature describes delayed emotional responses following ketamine infusions, particularly in individuals with trauma histories or chronic affective suppression [4,7,8]. These responses may reflect shifts in neural inhibition and emotional gating rather than reactions tied to the immediate treatment window [6].

Timing does not determine legitimacy. A delayed response is still a response.

# Session Five: Calm

By the fifth session, you may find yourself tracking changes. Mood. Sleep. Irritability. Focus. Comparisons start to form between how you feel now and how you felt before treatment began.

I noticed fewer sharp edges in daily life and a greater ease with emotional honesty, but no clear narrative of improvement. That ambiguity followed me into the room.

The fifth session itself was smooth and even. There were no intense images and no emotional spikes. Awareness felt spacious and quiet. Thoughts passed without attaching themselves to anything.

For the first time, the neutrality felt reassuring. Long-ignored tension seemed to unwind without drawing attention to itself.

Nothing demanded focus.

The dominant feeling afterward was calm.

That calm felt unfamiliar. I kept scanning it, waiting for the moment it would give way to restlessness or doubt. It didn't.

Sleep that night was light and broken, the kind where thoughts drift through without urgency. By morning, nothing felt lifted or solved, but the steadiness remained. I noticed myself moving through the day without bracing, without rehearsing conversations, without the low-level vigilance that had become background noise.

I caught myself trying to name what that meant, then stopped. Any label felt premature.

## After the Session

Calm can feel harder to trust than intensity.

When a session leaves you steady rather than activated, the most helpful response is often to let that steadiness be useful, rather than questioning it. Calm does not need to be explained to be real.

In the days that follow, it can help to:
- Attend to basic responsibilities without overthinking them
- Re-establish routines that previously felt heavy
- Notice reduced reactivity without trying to preserve it

Avoid testing calm by deliberately provoking difficult material.

## What Research Suggests

Repeated ketamine infusions are associated with cumulative changes in mood regulation rather than sudden or dramatic resolution [1,2,5]. Some patients report an increased gap between emotional stimulus and reaction, reflecting improved emotional regulation rather than emotional blunting [3,6].

These shifts can feel subtle and may not announce themselves as improvement [2,5]. Calm without a clear explanation has been documented as a treatment outcome, particularly later in a course of infusions [5,9].

# Session Six: Consolidation

The final session carries a different kind of pressure.

There is often an unspoken belief that the last treatment should conclude something, that it should deliver clarity, relief, or at least a sense of completion. I noticed a subtle urgency in myself, a desire to use the session well.

That urgency turned out to be unnecessary.

The sixth experience felt familiar in a way the earlier ones had not. Elements from previous sessions were present without competing for attention. Abstract movement from the first. Emotional tone from the second. Neutrality from the third. Bodily awareness from the fourth. Calm from the fifth.

Midway through the session, a few thoughts surfaced without effort. One was, **you are alive**. The other, **you are here in this moment**. Both arrived with a warmth that felt simple and unforced. Even now, remembering them brings a quiet swell of emotion rather than a story about what they meant.

Coming out of the final infusion, there was no dramatic shift. Instead, there was a grounded sense of being back in my body and in the room, oriented and present.

The question that followed was not What did this do? but What do I do next?

## After the Session

The end of a protocol is not an endpoint. It is a transition.

After the final session, attention often shifts away from experience and toward structure. That shift is appropriate. Consistency begins to matter more than introspection.

In the days and weeks that follow, it can help to:
- Maintain regular sleep and wake times
- Continue journaling at a pace that feels sustainable
- Schedule a follow-up conversation with your provider
- Pair any insight with ordinary, repeatable behavior

Avoid measuring success by emotional intensity. What persists quietly is often more important than what arrives dramatically.

## What Research Suggests

Clinical studies indicate that symptom improvement following ketamine treatment can persist or continue to evolve in the weeks after a completed protocol [2,5,9]. Neuroplastic changes associated with treatment do not immediately reverse once infusions stop [3,5].

Long-term outcomes vary, and maintenance strategies are individualized. Some patients pursue periodic booster sessions, while others rely on psychotherapy, medication adjustments, or lifestyle changes guided by a provider [5,10].

Ketamine opens a window. It does not determine what happens next [3,5].

# Work Between Sessions

Ketamine can act as a catalyst. What happens around it varies widely, and no amount of effort guarantees a particular outcome.

Between sessions, thoughts and feelings may surface with less resistance than usual. For me, writing helped slow that process down enough to notice what was there without having to organize or resolve it immediately. Before my first session, my thoughts often felt sealed off. After treatment began, they arrived more freely and with less effort. Writing gave them somewhere to land.

I did not write every day, and I did not try to make sense of everything. I stopped when the writing started to feel analytical or forced.

What follows are not instructions, just observations from my own experience:

- Write briefly, and stop before it becomes effortful
- You are not behind if answers do not arrive
- Periods that feel blank are still part of the process
- Some changes arrive quietly or later than expected
- Not all progress announces itself as insight

# Journaling Prompts

You do not need prompts to journal. If writing comes naturally, follow it.

If you feel stuck or unsure where to begin, these questions helped me notice patterns without forcing conclusions:

- What emotions or moods showed up without a clear reason, and how long did they last?
- Under what circumstances have I felt something similar before?
- What did my body register before my mind tried to explain it?
- What am I tempted to conclude too early about this experience?
- What feels even slightly less rigid or reactive than it did before treatment began?
- What happens if I allow this experience to remain unresolved for now?

# Closing Thoughts

Ketamine therapy is not a shortcut or a replacement for ongoing care. It is a tool that temporarily alters how the brain organizes experience. What follows from that window depends on many factors, including support, timing, and individual history.

Some people feel immediate relief. Others notice subtle change. Some feel unsettled before anything feels better. Some decide the treatment is not right for them. All of those outcomes are valid.

If this guide has done its job, it has not persuaded you of anything. It has simply kept you company through an unfamiliar process.

After six sessions, my main takeaway was not an answer, but a renewed respect for how much remains unknown. The mind is not a problem to be solved. It is something to pay attention to.

What you do with that attention belongs to you, and to the care you pursue next.

# References

1. Berman RM, Cappiello A, Anand A, et al. (2000). Antidepressant effects of ketamine in depressed patients. Biological Psychiatry, 47(4), 351–354.
https://doi.org/10.1016/S0006-3223(99)00230-9


2. Zarate CA Jr, Singh JB, Carlson PJ, et al. (2006). A randomized trial of an N-methyl-D-aspartate antagonist in treatment-resistant major depression. Archives of General Psychiatry, 63(8), 856–864.
https://doi.org/10.1001/archpsyc.63.8.856


3. Duman RS, Aghajanian GK. (2012). Synaptic dysfunction in depression: potential therapeutic targets. Science, 338(6103), 68–72.
https://doi.org/10.1126/science.1222939


4. Feder A, Parides MK, Murrough JW, et al. (2014). Efficacy of intravenous ketamine for treatment of chronic posttraumatic stress disorder. JAMA Psychiatry, 71(6), 681–688.
https://doi.org/10.1001/jamapsychiatry.2014.62


5. Krystal JH, Abdallah CG, Sanacora G, et al. (2019). Ketamine and the potential role of neuroplasticity in treatment-resistant depression. Neuropsychopharmacology, 44, 178–193.
https://doi.org/10.1038/s41386-018-0208-8

6. Duman RS, Sanacora G, Krystal JH. (2019). Altered connectivity and synaptic plasticity in depression and rapid-acting antidepressant responses. Molecular Psychiatry, 24, 27–38.
https://doi.org/10.1038/s41380-018-0155-7

7. Wilkinson ST, Ballard ED, Bloch MH, et al. (2018). The effect of a single dose of intravenous ketamine on trauma-related emotional processing. Journal of Affective Disorders, 241, 519–526.
https://doi.org/10.1016/j.jad.2018.08.056

8. Schatzberg AF. (2019).
A word to the wise about ketamine. American Journal of Psychiatry, 176(6), 422–424.
https://doi.org/10.1176/appi.ajp.2019.19040415

9. Phillips JL, Norris S, Talbot J, et al. (2019).
Single and repeated ketamine infusions for reduction of suicidal ideation in treatment-resistant depression. Journal of Psychopharmacology, 33(12), 1476–1486.
https://doi.org/10.1177/0269881119887557

10. Wilkinson ST, Sanacora G, Bloch MH. (2017).
Ketamine: A potential rapid-acting antisuicidal agent? Depression and Anxiety, 34(8), 711–717.
https://doi.org/10.1002/da.22678

# About the Author

Patrick Diedrich is a writer and editor with a background in U.S. Army service and operational leadership in high-stress environments. He served as a senior non-commissioned officer, with experience in decision-making under conditions of uncertainty.

His work focuses on resilience, preparedness, and human performance, particularly how individuals and systems adapt under sustained stress. His writing has been published and distributed internationally.

This book reflects both personal experience and a professional interest in how medical and psychological interventions interact with cognition, emotional regulation, and long-term functioning. It is written with respect for clinical boundaries and the role of qualified providers in patient care.

www.ingramcontent.com/pod-product-compliance
Lightning Source LLC
Chambersburg PA
CBHW070051070426
42449CB00012BA/3224